Descriptive and Narrative Writing

Language Arts

Grades
3–5

KING ARTHUR'S
ACADEMY

Suzanna E. Henshon, Ph.D.
Illustrated by Jon Compton

Copyright ©2007 Prufrock Press Inc.

Edited by Lacy Elwood
Editorial Assistant: Kate Sepanski
Production Design by Marjorie Parker
Illustrations by Jon Compton

ISBN-13: 978-1-59363-221-2
ISBN-10: 1-59363-221-5

Prufrock Press Inc.
P.O. Box 8813
Waco, TX 76714-8813
Phone: (800) 998-2208
Fax: (800) 240-0333
http://www.prufrock.com

DEDICATION

This book is dedicated to my nephews, William Henshon, Mark Henshon, and James Henshon. May their lives be filled with creativity and adventure.

CONTENTS

DEDICATION 3

ACKNOWLEDGEMENTS 7

TEACHER'S GUIDE 8

A LETTER TO THE ADMISSIONS OFFICE 9

THE ACCEPTANCE LETTER 10

PACKING FOR SCHOOL 12

A TRIP TO THE KNIGHT & BEAST DEPARTMENT STORE 13

A STROLL THROUGH KNIGHT & BEAST DEPARTMENT STORE 14

TRAVELING TO KING ARTHUR'S ACADEMY 15

ARRIVING AT KING ARTHUR'S ACADEMY 17

DECORATING YOUR DORMITORY ROOM 18

DRESSING FOR ASSEMBLY 20

THE GRAND TOUR 21

WRITING A PAGE FOR THE COURSE CATALOG 22

SWORD-SWINGING ADVENTURE 23

THE KNIGHTS OF THE ROUND TABLE 24

RECESS 25

A LECTURE WITH MERLIN 26

A GUEST APPEARANCE BY ARTHUR XV AND QUEEN GUINEVERE XV 27

THE BOOK OF MERLIN: A BOOK REPORT 28

DECORATING YOUR SHIELD 30

DESIGNING YOUR OWN SWORD 31

FUN AND GAMES 33

A CLOSE ENCOUNTER WITH KING ARTHUR'S GHOST 34

THE SWORD-THROWING CONTEST 36

THE DRAGON IN THE MOAT 37

LADY ELAINE'S MIRROR 38

MERLIN'S WAND 39

THE FAMOUS STONE 40

AN ADDITION TO THE CASTLE 42

A BOOK SIGNING 43

AN AFTERNOON OF READING 44

STUDENT COUNCIL ELECTIONS   45

WRITING THE SCHOOL SONG   46

THE ACTIVITIES FAIR   47

COMPETING AGAINST THE MORDRED SCHOOL   48

THE MAP OF TARTORIA   49

STUDYING FOR YOUR EXAM   50

MESSAGE IN A BOTTLE   51

KING ARTHUR'S STATUE   52

THE CROWN OF GUINEVERE   53

YEARBOOK SUPERLATIVES AT KING ARTHUR'S ACADEMY   54

THE PET DRAGON   55

BEHIND THE ACADEMY WALLS   56

THE REPORT CARD   57

THE FINAL AWARDS CEREMONY   58

WRITING YOUR MEMOIR   59

RUBRIC FOR WRITING EXERCISES   60

RUBRIC FOR DRAWING EXERCISES   61

RESOURCES   62

ABOUT THE AUTHOR   63

ACKNOWLEDGEMENTS

Many of the ideas I used to create this book were inspired by my studies at the College of William and Mary in Virginia under the direction of Dr. Joyce VanTassel-Baska. Joyce's creativity in teaching and writing set a wonderful example, one that I have tried to bring to my own students at Florida Gulf Coast University, where I teach writing to dual-enrollment learners. I would also like to thank my parents, Thomas and Elaine Henshon, for their support of this project. Lacy Elwood and Joel McIntosh of Prufrock Press provided wonderful encouragement and support during the editing and publication process.

TEACHER'S GUIDE

King Arthur's Academy: Descriptive and Narrative Writing Exercises is designed to help students develop stories and ideas that they can enjoy for many years to come. This activity book has been written for high-potential and high-ability learners, but can also be used in the general classroom. *King Arthur's Academy* offers activities for advanced learners in language arts and general enrichment.

In the ideal situation, all students in a class will have copies of *King Arthur's Academy* to use as workbooks during the course of a school term. At the end of the school year, each student will have a book to take home to share with his or her parents. This achievement will provide a stronger link between home and school learning. In a homeschool situation, a child might work on these exercises for several weeks, eventually creating his or her own collection of stories.

King Arthur's Academy is student-friendly. The activities are intentionally written with open endings within a reasonable amount of restriction, because, after testing open-ended activities with high-ability learners, I have discovered that they lead to a variety of creative responses that might not be possible if the children are forced to write within certain restrictions. However, at the same time, some level of direction is provided to the students, so that the students do not feel lost and have an idea of which way they should respond to the open-ended prompt. *King Arthur's Academy* is also teacher-friendly. The activities do not require teacher instructions or an answer key, and students may work at their own pace during class time. Because the prompts do have some direction (e.g., asking students to write a story, draw a picture, or prepare a proposal), it is easy for teachers to assess the students' work. A general writing assessment rubric and a general drawing assessment rubric are included at the end of this book.

King Arthur's Academy follows Texas Essential Knowledge and Skills standards and benchmarks in the area of English and language arts, and these standards are applicable in many other states. In grades 3–5, students are expected to solve problems, appreciate literature, interpret and evaluate, respond appropriately and courteously to directions and questions, connect experiences and ideas, and compare language and oral traditions (family stories) that reflect customs, regions, and cultures. With this activity book, students will fulfill state standards and benchmarks as they write to entertain (e.g., as they compose various short stories, poems, and other works).

When a student comes to you and asks for more creative writing challenge, you can direct him or her toward *King Arthur's Academy*. The enrichment activities in this book, appropriate for grades 3–5, have shown remarkable results with learners of varying ability levels. Happy writing!

A LETTER TO THE ADMISSIONS OFFICE

As you tour King Arthur's Academy one day, you become very excited about applying for admission. After all, who wouldn't want to attend school in a castle that has a real moat and huge dragons? And, at what other academy do students have the opportunity to wear armor to class? You are enchanted by the tour, during which you see famous alumni portraits on the wall (including one of Sir Lancelot), and you immediately decide to write a letter to the admissions office. Think about what you can contribute to the campus and why you want to attend King Arthur's Academy. Then, write a letter that is sure to reserve you a place as a student behind the castle walls.

_____

_____

_____

_____

_____

_____

_____

_____

_____

_____

_____

_____

_____

_____

THE ACCEPTANCE LETTER

One day a flying sword arrives in your front lawn (upsetting your mother's gardenias). Noticing the seal of King Arthur's Academy imprinted on the sword, you desperately hope the attached letter bears good news.

~ K.A.A. ~

Dear Student,

Congratulations! We are pleased to offer you admission to study at King Arthur's Academy.

Please pick up the following books:

The Art of Sword Dipping,   The History of Camelot,
Finding the Holy Grail,   I am Guinevere,
How to Win Battles & Influence People

Also remember to bring the following:

A single-edged sword,   A sword handle (dipped in silver),
A saddle (finest leather),   A suit of armor (adjustable)

Please let us know if you plan to attend King Arthur's Academy this fall. We hope to see you then.

Yours truly,

Lancelot Lake

Admissions Officer

King Arthur's Academy

THE ACCEPTANCE LETTER

You're excited to receive the admissions letter, but now you wonder how to send your reply—by sword or through traditional mail? Explain your decision, and then write your response letter to the academy.

_____

_____

_____

_____

_____

_____

_____

_____

_____

_____

_____

_____

_____

_____

_____

_____

_____

_____

_____

PACKING FOR SCHOOL

Oh, boy! You're taking off for school in 3 days, and you have not yet begun to pack. What will you bring with you? The sword from the basement (slightly rusty)? Your favorite book, *The Camelot Letters*? A new shield (if you can afford it)? In this exercise, describe the challenges you face and the decisions you make as you pack your bags for a life at King Arthur's Academy. Make a list of what you pack and explain why you've chosen each item.

_____

_____

_____

_____

_____

_____

_____

_____

_____

_____

_____

_____

_____

_____

_____

_____

_____

_____

A TRIP TO THE KNIGHT & BEAST DEPARTMENT STORE

You like to shop and always have fun visiting department stores. You decide to visit the Knight & Beast Department Store for your school supplies. Draw a picture of what the store looks like, including its famous window displays.

A STROLL THROUGH KNIGHT & BEAST DEPARTMENT STORE

As you stroll through the Knight & Beast Department Store, you see swords of all shapes and sizes—from chocolate swords (they look delicious!) to triple-edged swords that leap off the counter and into your hand. You also see ancient texts on the wall, including *How to Win the Heart of a Prince or Princess*, *What Not to Do When You Encounter a Dragon*, and *Is Magic a Myth? True Encounters With Merlin the Wizard*.

"Can I help you?" a salesperson asks, and you nod. You pull out your list of items, and the salesperson points you in the right direction. Below, write a journal entry about your shopping experiences.

_____

_____

_____

_____

_____

_____

_____

_____

_____

_____

_____

_____

_____

_____

_____

_____

_____

TRAVELING TO
KING ARTHUR'S ACADEMY

Wanting to arrive at King Arthur's Academy as quickly as possible, you decide to wait in line for a free ride on the back of a dragon (flying is so much faster than driving). As you wait somewhat nervously for your turn, you examine the three dragons giving rides. Which one will you pick to carry you high in the sky? One that blows smoke, or one that blows bubbles? Which color dragon do you like best? Describe the creature you choose for your ride, from the feel of its skin to its personality.

TRAVELING TO
KING ARTHUR'S ACADEMY

_____

_____

_____

_____

_____

_____

_____

_____

_____

_____

_____

_____

_____

_____

_____

_____

_____

_____

_____

_____

_____

_____

ARRIVING AT KING ARTHUR'S ACADEMY

Flying through the air atop your dragon, you look down and see an amazing turreted castle—King Arthur's Academy! Among other buildings, there's a huge hall, dormitories, a recreational sword field, and a mysterious building that you cannot identify. There's also a moat surrounding the entire castle complex, and you see a dragon swimming in its dark water. Draw a map of the school, and carefully label each building, from the huge hall that holds the Round Table to the dragon-filled moat!

DECORATING YOUR DORMITORY ROOM

Upon arriving at King Arthur's Academy, your first stop is Excalibur Landing, the dormitory for all first-year students. Eager to see your room, you walk down the hall and enter the last door on the right. Although the room is somewhat small and very plain, you know that you can make yourself feel right at home if you fix it up with the right decorations. So, how will you decorate your room? Draw a picture of your room, from the posters on the walls to the headboard on your bed. Then, write a letter home to your friends describing your room.

DECORATING YOUR DORMITORY ROOM

_____
_____
_____
_____
_____
_____
_____
_____
_____
_____
_____
_____
_____
_____
_____
_____
_____
_____
_____
_____
_____

DRESSING FOR ASSEMBLY

The first student assembly will take place in 15 minutes, but as a first-year student, you're not quite sure what to wear. Do students dress up with caps and gowns, or do they wear jeans and carry swords? You'd better decide on something quickly, because it's almost time to go! Draw a picture of yourself in the clothes you choose to wear to your first official event at King Arthur's Academy, and then write a paragraph explaining why you chose these clothes.

_____

_____

_____

_____

_____

_____

_____

_____

_____

_____

_____

THE GRAND TOUR

Before the first classes of the day have begun, you nervously follow the other first-year students on a tour led by 16-year-old Sir Lancelyn Knight. "Hello," he says, "and welcome to King Arthur's Academy. On this tour, you will see why we are the alma mater of some of the world's most famous knights. Please follow me." Below, write and illustrate a minibrochure for King Arthur's Academy, based on the sites you see on your tour of the academy.

WRITING A PAGE FOR
THE COURSE CATALOG

What are your classes like? It's time for your first class of the day: "The History of Archery." As you wait for your teacher to arrive, you and several other students talk excitedly about the topics you think this class will cover. The flight of an arrow, perhaps?

Your second class at the academy is titled, "Damsels in Distress." You will be studying glamorous princesses and other resourceful damsels who made history, including Sleeping Beauty, Cinderella, and princesses who have yet to be discovered by the fairyland media. Can you convince other students (even the boys) that this is a class worth taking?

Your third class, "Famous Feats and Myths," is down the hallway past the portrait of the Disappearing Merlin. As you stroll along, Merlin steps out of the portrait and directs you to the Golden Horse Room, where you will learn about the accomplishments of knights and ladies in medieval days.

Write an exciting course description of at least one of these classes for the school's course catalog that will make every student at King Arthur's Academy want to take these classes.

_____

_____

_____

_____

_____

_____

_____

_____

_____

_____

SWORD-SWINGING ADVENTURE

Your fourth class, "How to Swing a Sword," is a real workout! As one might expect, you spend a lot of time practicing the proper way to swing a sword. How good of a knight are you? When you swing your sword, do you ever miss your target? Have any serious accidents ever happened in class? Write a poem about the sword-swinging adventures of you and your classmates on this first day of class.

_____

_____

_____

_____

_____

_____

_____

_____

_____

_____

_____

_____

_____

_____

_____

_____

THE KNIGHTS OF THE ROUND TABLE

"Knights of the Round Table" is your fifth class of the day, during which you spend a lot of time learning about Lancelot and heroes of the Round Table, studying battle scenes, and even reenacting a few famous moments from Arthurian literature. Write a one-page essay about one of the knights or one of the experiences of the knights. This will take some historical research on your part.

_____

_____

_____

_____

_____

_____

_____

_____

_____

_____

_____

_____

_____

_____

_____

_____

_____

_____

_____

_____

RECESS

It's time to take a break from class, and you can't wait to have a breath of fresh air. Stepping outside, you see a group of kids playing with flying swords in one area of the playground, while other children board the Dragon-Go-Round. What will you do at recess? What sort of adventures will you have? Write a letter to a friend back home describing some of the activities you can choose to take part in.

_____

_____

_____

_____

_____

_____

_____

_____

_____

_____

_____

_____

_____

_____

_____

_____

_____

_____

A LECTURE WITH MERLIN

You have read stories about Merlin and know he's an amazing magician, so you're excited to find out that he'll be lecturing at King Arthur's Academy. What will he talk about? With careful thought, develop a flier to advertise this upcoming event. Provide detailed and exciting information describing what Merlin will discuss. Note that fliers use more text than posters, which generally have lots of graphics.

A GUEST APPEARANCE BY ARTHUR XV AND QUEEN GUINEVERE XV

As an academy student, you are aware of King Arthur's influence. The academy is, after all, named after this famous medieval figure. Today you have an exciting opportunity: Arthur XV, a direct descendant of the legendary boy who drew the sword from the stone, will visit campus. You are lucky enough to attend a luncheon with this young man, and to also meet his lovely bride. Queen Guinevere XV is a direct descendant of the legendary Guinevere and is said to bear a striking resemblance to her beautiful ancestor. It's even rumored that Queen Guinevere XV has the diary of the original Guinevere in her possession. What will Arthur and Guinevere talk about? What questions will you ask? You will be writing an interview for the school newspaper, so write questions to ask either Arthur or Guinevere below.

_____

_____

_____

_____

_____

_____

_____

_____

_____

_____

_____

_____

_____

_____

THE BOOK OF MERLIN: A BOOK REPORT

As a student, you are assigned to write a book report on Ralston Fallstaff's *The Book of Merlin*. You can't wait to flip through this ancient, dust-covered volume, which is more than 1,000 years old, because it's rumored that young Arthur held this very book in his hand. You can hardly believe that the heroic king read the same pages at which you are now gazing. Write a book report about the book and then draw the cover of this mysterious volume on the next page.

_____

_____

_____

_____

_____

_____

_____

_____

_____

_____

_____

_____

_____

_____

_____

_____

THE BOOK OF MERLIN: A BOOK REPORT

DECORATING YOUR SHIELD

Now that you are a knight-in-training, you finally have your very own shield. Draw your shield, complete with all its symbolic markings. Is it covered with scenes from your hometown or with medieval heroes? Whatever the case, remember that no one else in the world will have a shield exactly like yours, so handle the assignment with care!

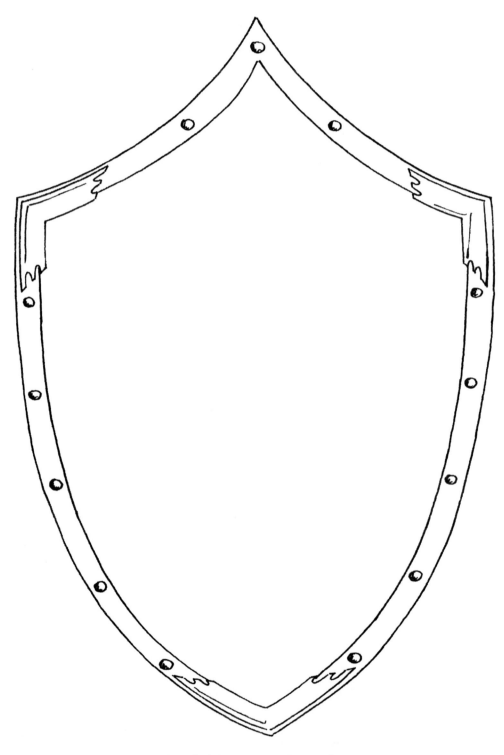

DESIGNING YOUR OWN SWORD

You never held a sword in your hands before you came to King Arthur's Academy, and now you have the opportunity to design a sword of your very own! "Think carefully," older students advise you, "Because this is a once-in-a-lifetime opportunity. You will have this sword for years." With these words in mind, you sit down and begin sketching your ideas. Will it have a double-edge? Will it be extremely long? Draw a picture of your sword, using the hilt below as a starting point, and then write a paragraph about its unique features.

DESIGN YOUR OWN SWORD

_____

_____

_____

_____

_____

_____

_____

_____

_____

_____

_____

_____

_____

_____

_____

_____

_____

_____

_____

_____

_____

_____

_____

_____

_____

FUN AND GAMES

One day as you stroll down the hall, you come across someone playing a video game in one of the rooms. As you watch curiously, you realize that the games at King Arthur's Academy are unlike any of the games you've ever played before. Design your own video game about life at the academy. What will you call your game? What special features will it have? The world is waiting to play your game, so let your imagination run free as you create a game that no one has ever experienced before. Write a proposal to a video game company describing the features of your game and telling the company why it should create and sell your product.

_____

_____

_____

_____

_____

_____

_____

_____

_____

_____

_____

_____

_____

_____

_____

A CLOSE ENCOUNTER WITH KING ARTHUR'S GHOST

Since your first days at the academy, you've heard stories about King Arthur's ghost roaming the halls at night. However, you are skeptical about these stories. After all, ghosts don't really exist, right? That's what you think—until an apparition of the king glides by! What is it doing, and where is it going? Gather your courage to become a ghost investigator, and write a suspenseful story about your adventures hunting down King Arthur's ghost.

_____

_____

_____

_____

_____

_____

_____

_____

_____

_____

_____

_____

_____

_____

_____

_____

_____

_____

_____

A CLOSE ENCOUNTER WITH KING ARTHUR'S GHOST

_____

_____

_____

_____

_____

_____

_____

_____

_____

_____

_____

_____

                              _____

                              _____

                              _____

                              _____

                              _____

                              _____

                              _____

                         _____

THE SWORD-THROWING CONTEST

Since arriving at King Arthur's Academy, you've been studying the size, structure, and lethal abilities of swords. You know that swords can be downright dangerous, but nevertheless, you can't resist a little friendly competition. You've decided to enter the sword-throwing contest. For this contest, you must develop your own amazing routine that will win maximum points from the judges. With so much at stake, your routine must be entertaining, slightly dangerous, and—most importantly—absolutely flawless! Give an account of the competition (who were the winners?), and tell us what you did to impress the judges.

_____

_____

_____

_____

_____

_____

_____

_____

_____

_____

_____

_____

_____

_____

_____

_____

_____

_____

NAME:_____ DATE:_____

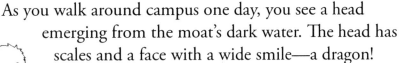

THE DRAGON IN THE MOAT

As you walk around campus one day, you see a head emerging from the moat's dark water. The head has scales and a face with a wide smile—a dragon!

"Hi, there," you say. "How's life in the moat?"

"Pretty good . . . at least for the past 600 years."

"Great," you say.

"Would you like my business card?" the dragon asks. "This way you'll know how to reach me if ever you need my assistance." He hands you a business card with his picture on it, then climbs out of the moat and flies away.

You can't believe your eyes. You didn't know that dragons have cards, just like baseball players! In the space below, draw a picture of the dragon and list a few vital statistics, including the dragon's name, weight, number of scales, special skills, and the number of treasures it currently guards.

LADY ELAINE'S MIRROR

Wandering through the hall one day, you notice a mirror with a golden frame and plaque beneath it that reads, "Lady Elaine's Mirror." Curious as usual, you decide to peek into the unusual glass. What do you see? Yourself? Someone else? The future? Write a conversation between you and your best friend at the academy, telling him or her about the vision you see and what you think it means.

_____

_____

_____

_____

_____

_____

_____

_____

_____

_____

_____

_____

_____

_____

_____

_____

MERLIN'S WAND

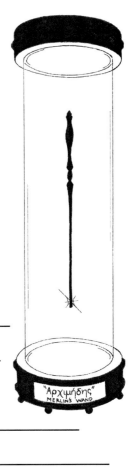

In the school archives rests a wand in a glass case. Labeled "Merlin's Wand," the shiny black stick sparkles faintly when you look at it. For a moment, you imagine the wand has flown into your hand, but when you look again, you see it still sparkles in its case. What would it be like to have this wand for a single afternoon? What would you do with it? Would you use it to complete your homework? To create a never-ending supply of chocolate chip cookies? To find the elusive Holy Grail? Write an adventure story describing what you would do if you could use the magic wand for one day and one day only!

_____

_____

_____

_____

_____

_____

_____

_____

_____

_____

_____

_____

_____

_____

THE FAMOUS STONE

One day the entire academy takes a field trip—on horseback, of course—to a surprise destination. After dismounting your horse, you look down to see a stone that has a hole on top and the following inscription on its side:

HERE IS WHERE YOUNG ARTHUR
DREW THE SWORD FROM THE STONE
AND BECAME
KING OF ENGLAND.

Gazing at the stone, you feel as if you are going back in time, and you can't help but shiver. What was it like for Arthur to pull a sword from this stone that no one else could lift? How would it feel for a humble servant to suddenly become the royal King of England? In this exercise, write a story from Arthur's point of view about that fateful day.

_____

_____

_____

_____

_____

_____

_____

_____

_____

_____

_____

_____

THE FAMOUS STONE

_____

_____

_____

_____

_____

_____

_____

_____

_____

_____

_____

_____

_____

_____

_____

HERE ARTHUR BECAME KING

_____

_____

_____

_____

_____

_____

AN ADDITION TO THE CASTLE

King Arthur's Academy is undergoing some renovations. The board of trustees would like the latest addition to the school to be a turreted tower that can be seen for miles around. Tonight they plan to have a meeting that students, staff, and faculty can attend to share ideas about the new tower, named for Sir Kay (King Arthur's brother). What should the tower be used for? How tall should it be? Who will be allowed to go inside? Now is your opportunity to make a difference, so make sure your ideas are heard! Below, write a speech about your ideas for the tower's design and use to make to the students, faculty, and staff at the Academy.

_____

_____

_____

_____

_____

_____

_____

_____

_____

_____

_____

_____

_____

_____

_____

_____

A BOOK SIGNING

To your excitement, you see a poster advertising a book signing by Mordred X, your favorite rock star. What does this poster look like? And, what is the name of his upcoming book? Draw the poster that is catching everyone's attention, and be sure to include a description of Mordred's new book.

AN AFTERNOON OF READING

In study hall one day, you notice a comic book that has been left on a nearby table. The comic book, *The Knights of the Square Table*, appears to be a parody of the adventures of the Knights of the Round Table. As you flip through the book, you can't help but laugh. Some scenes are so funny that you're sure you'll remember them for a long time. You decide to write a review for your school paper. Share your favorite parts of the comic book with your readers and convince them that this is one book they'll definitely have to check out!

_____

_____

_____

_____

_____

_____

_____

_____

_____

_____

_____

_____

_____

_____

_____

STUDENT COUNCIL ELECTIONS

As a first-year student, you decide to run for student council, which means you'll need to create some campaign posters. Think about how you will market yourself—as a diligent student in archery class, or as someone who is always on the mark when hurtling swords? Draw a campaign poster and create a slogan that will convince other students that voting for you will add to the illustrious history of King Arthur's Academy.

WRITING THE SCHOOL SONG

All students at King Arthur's Academy have been invited to come up with a new school song. The student whose song is chosen will receive a year of free tuition and will have his or her name written in the school's history books. Now is the time to show your school spirit! Write a school song that can be sung at games and assemblies, a song that reflects the long and illustrious history of the academy and promotes school spirit. Students at King Arthur's Academy take pride in their school—so write a song that everyone will be proud to sing.

_____

_____

_____

_____

_____

_____

_____

_____

_____

_____

_____

_____

_____

_____

_____

_____

THE ACTIVITIES FAIR

Walking into the Great Hall one morning, you are surprised to see torches and large banners. Then you remember that today is the activities fair. Dozens of clubs at King Arthur's Academy have set up booths to provide information for potential members. As you walk around the room with other interested students, think about which clubs you will join. The Swashbuckling Knights? The Camelot Comedy Club? The Ladies of the Sword? The Treasure Hunters? Below, create a colorful flier for a club that is trying to attract new members.

COMPETING AGAINST
THE MORDRED SCHOOL

One of the biggest rivalries of King Arthur's Academy is The Mordred School. Tomorrow students from both schools will compete in a jousting match, so tonight King Arthur's Academy will have a big pep rally (complete with bonfires, dragons, and waving swords) to fire up the students and prepare them for victory. There are no cheerleaders at King Arthur's Academy; instead, students take turns leading songs and chants that they have written themselves. This week you and your friends want to take a special part in the pep rally. Write a song or a chant that will encourage those competing in tomorrow's match to defeat your opponents from The Mordred School.

_____

_____

_____

_____

_____

_____

_____

_____

_____

_____

_____

_____

_____

_____

THE MAP OF TARTORIA

During history class your professor takes you to the school archives and points out an ancient map of Tartoria. "This map predates the founding of the school," he explains. "Many believe that it leads to treasure." In the space below, draw a copy of this ancient map—complete with long-forgotten castles, sea creatures, and fire-breathing dragons. Be sure and label the places on your map. After all, you never know when a map like this could come in handy!

STUDYING FOR YOUR EXAM

One rainy morning, your professor announces that everyone must begin studying for the final exam in "Famous Feats and Medieval Myths." You have only the textbook, your notes, and your mental abilities to help you prepare for this test. Develop a logical plan for what you will study and when you will study it. You only have one week to prepare. Go ahead and write your study plan in the calendar below.

SUNDAY	
MONDAY	
TUESDAY	
WEDNESDAY	
THURSDAY	
FRIDAY	
SATURDAY	

MESSAGE IN A BOTTLE

One sunny afternoon you are sailing a handmade boat in the moat and talking with the dragon when you see a glass bottle floating by. Noticing a piece of paper inside the bottle, you can't help but wonder what it could be. Should you grab the bottle and pull out the paper? Explain what you do next and what happens as a result.

_____

_____

_____

_____

_____

_____

_____

_____

_____

_____

_____

_____

_____

KING ARTHUR'S STATUE

A generous benefactor has donated money to the school to be used for a statue of King Arthur. You've been selected to be part of the special committee that will help design the statue. You must first research ancient to modern-day depictions of Arthur and then present a dynamic design of the legendary king to the committee. The design for the statue not only has to be approved by the headmaster and board of trustees, but it must be one that will stand the test of time. Think carefully before you draw, and then create a design that will be sure to impress the committee and honor King Arthur. After drawing your design, write a caption explaining to the committee why you chose to depict Arthur the way you did.

THE CROWN OF GUINEVERE

For months an archaeological excavation has been going on at the academy, and one day you hear exciting news: The crown of the legendary Guinevere has been discovered behind the walls of Founders Hall! Everyone at King Arthur's Academy is very excited. Write a story for *The Sword & Stone Times*, the school newspaper, about this legendary crown and how it was found.

_____

_____

_____

_____

_____

_____

_____

_____

_____

_____

_____

_____

_____

_____

_____

_____

_____

_____

YEARBOOK SUPERLATIVES
AT KING ARTHUR'S ACADEMY

Students at King Arthur's Academy always await the yearbook with anticipation. The pictures are funny and memorable, but the best part is reading which students earned honors and titles. Your job as a member of the journalism team is to come up with at least five yearbook superlatives, such as Most Likely to Dual a Dragon, Least Likely to Rescue a Fair Maiden, and Most Popular Knight-in-Training. Use your imagination to make this the best and funniest yearbook yet!

1. _____

_____

2. _____

_____

3. _____

_____

4. _____

_____

5. _____

_____

THE PET DRAGON

One day you see a little dragon crawling feebly through the fields where students usually practice throwing their swords. The dragon, which appears to be stressed, has a broken wing. Write a journal entry about your first week tending the dragon. What it is like to have a pet dragon? Where did this dragon come from and what has happened to it? What does he or she like to eat and play with? How big is he or she?

_____

_____

_____

_____

_____

_____

_____

_____

_____

_____

_____

_____

_____

_____

_____

_____

_____

_____

BEHIND THE ACADEMY WALLS

One rainy day you decide to explore Founders Hall with a group of friends, because everyone is dying to know what lies behind the elegant walls and poised portraits. What mysteries will be uncovered at the academy? Like a detective, you take your curiosity and a flashlight, and you begin wandering the dimly lit halls when you mysteriously wind up behind the walls of Founders Hall. Write a suspenseful tale of what you find behind the walls to tell your friends when you get back to your dorm.

_____

_____

_____

_____

_____

_____

_____

_____

_____

_____

_____

_____

_____

_____

_____

_____

_____

THE REPORT CARD

You've finally taken the last of your exams, and now you wait with anticipation for your final grades. Hopefully all of your hard work has paid off! Create your own report card on the scroll below. Be sure to list your classes, grades, and any comments you might have received from your instructors.

THE FINAL AWARDS CEREMONY

As the school year ends at King Arthur's Academy, the time has finally come for students to empty their lockers, pack their trunks, and head home. Before students leave, they must attend the final awards ceremony of the year. Describe the awards ceremony. Write a speech that the director of the school will give to the students, celebrating the exciting year.

_____

_____

_____

_____

_____

_____

_____

_____

_____

_____

_____

_____

_____

_____

_____

_____

_____

WRITING YOUR MEMOIR

Heading home for a summer break full of pool parties and lemonade, you stop and wonder, "Should I write a book about my experiences at school?" You suddenly realize that Knightly Press hasn't published a first-person memoir of a student at King Arthur's Academy since Lancelot's *I Was a Young Knight: The Story of Lancelot*—but that was written centuries ago! You decide to write a memoir and try to think of the perfect title for your story. *Once Upon a Time: The Story of a First-Year Academy Student? How I Learned to Swing Swords?* Think of a great title, and write a proposal letter to the publishing company describing the book idea and discussing the highlights of the year that will make good chapters.

_____

_____

_____

_____

_____

_____

_____

_____

_____

_____

_____

_____

_____

_____

_____

_____

RUBRIC FOR WRITING EXERCISES

Below is a sample of a writing rubric for grades 3–5 that can be used to assess the writing activities in this book. In this rubric, points are left blank, for teachers to fill in according to their own grading schemes. Teachers may make copies of this rubric to assess the multiple writing activities in this book.

Activity Title: _____

	Superb (___ points)	Adept (___ points)	Unacceptable (____ points)
Organization	Writing is clear and coherent; Presentation is neat; Ideas are organized very clearly for maximum understanding.	Writing is mostly clear and coherent, but does have some parts that are difficult to understand; Presentation could be neater; Ideas are organized clearly.	Writing is not clear or coherent; Presentation is sloppy; Ideas are not organized clearly.
Content	Material is imaginative, creative, and descriptive; Prompt is addressed accurately; Student demonstrates understanding of the task assigned.	Material could use more imagination, creativity, or description; Prompt is addressed appropriately; Student demonstrates some understanding of the task assigned, but could use review.	Material is not imaginative, creative, or descriptive; Prompt is not addressed; Student's content is inappropriate for the classroom; Student does not demonstrate understanding of the assigned task.
Vocabulary	Student uses advanced vocabulary and demonstrates understanding of its meaning; Student uses appropriate word choice.	Student uses some advanced vocabulary, but does not always demonstrate an understanding of its meaning; Student uses appropriate word choice; Some misuse of words or phrases.	Student does not used advanced vocabulary; Student does not use appropriate word choice; Student often misuses words and phrases.

Total Points: _____

RUBRIC FOR DRAWING EXERCISES

Below is a sample of a drawing rubric for grades 3–5 that can be used to assess the drawing activities in this book. In this rubric, points are left blank, for teachers to fill in according to their own grading schemes. Teachers may make copies of this rubric to assess the multiple drawing activities in this book.

Activity Title: _____

	Superb (___ points)	Adept (___ points)	Unacceptable (___ points)
Skill	Shows advanced drawing capabilities; Ideas are clearly conveyed through pictures; Drawing is neat.	Work shows appropriate artistic skills for age; Ideas could be clearer; Drawing is somewhat messy.	Poorly drawn; Ideas are not conveyed through work; Drawing is sloppy.
Content	Drawing is imaginative, creative, and descriptive; Prompt is addressed accurately; Student demonstrates understanding of the task assigned.	Drawing could use more imagination, creativity, or description; Prompt is addressed appropriately; Student demonstrates some understanding of the task assigned, but could use review.	Drawing is not imaginative, creative, or descriptive; Prompt is not addressed; Student's content is inappropriate for the classroom; Student does not demonstrate understanding of the assigned task.

Total Points: _____

RESOURCES

Byan, M. (2004). *Arms and armor: DK eyewitness books series.* New York: DK Publishing.

Carlson, L. (1998). *Days of knights and damsels: An activity guide.* Chicago: Chicago Review Press.

De Angeli, M. (1998). *The door in the wall.* New York: Random House Children's Books.

Gray, E. (1987). *Adam of the road.* New York: Penguin.

Green, R. L., & Green, R. T. (1998). *King Arthur and his knights of the roundtable.* New York: Penguin Group.

Gravett, C., & Dann, G.(2004). *Knight: DK eyewitness book series.* New York: DK Publishing.

Hindley, J. (2003). *Knights & castles: The Usborne time traveller series.* New York: Usborne Publishing.

Maynard, C. (1998). *Eyewitness readers: Days of the knights: A tale of castles and battles.* New York: DK Publishing.

McGovern, A., & Andreasen, D. (2001). *If you lived in the days of the knights.* New York: Scholastic.

Murrell, D. (2005). *The best book of knights and castles.* Boston: Houghton Mifflin.

O'Brien, P. (1998). *The making of a knight.* Boston: Charlesbridge Publishing.

Osborne, W., & Osborne, M. P. (2000). *Knights and castles: A nonfiction companion to The Knight at Dawn.* New York: Random House.

Scieszka, J. (1991). *Knights of the kitchen table: Time warp trio.* New York: Viking.

Starr, F. (2006). *Castle and knight.* New York: DK Publishing.

Sutcliff, R., & Malory, T. (1994). *Sword & the circle: King Arthur and the knights of the roundtable.* New York: Penguin Young Readers Group.

Twain, M. (2001). *A Connecticut yankee in King Arthur's court.* New York: Dover Publications.

Whalen, M. (2006). *The king of Attolia.* New York: HarperCollins Children's Books.

White, T. H. (1993). *The sword in the stone.* New York: Penguin.

Yolen, J. (2004). *Sword of the rightful king: A novel of King Arthur.* New York: Harcourt Children's Books.

ABOUT THE AUTHOR

Suzanna E. Henshon graduated from The College of William and Mary with a Ph.D. in gifted education in 2005 and currently teaches full-time at Florida Gulf Coast University in Fort Myers. She is the author of *Mildew on the Wall* (2004) and *Spiders on the Ceiling* (2006), both published by Royal Fireworks Press.

CPSIA information can be obtained at www.ICGtesting.com
Printed in the USA
BVOW051141150512

290276BV00003B/1/P